.

Author photo taken at

The Old Gate

Hebden Bridge

By Mike Stobart

GREEN FLAG

CONFESSIONS OF A CAR BREAKDOWN

CALL CENTRE

BY

MICHAEL O'BRIEN

Going live at Green Flag

I'd worked in a call centre once before at the Bradford and Bingley building Society. I was a mortgage 'advisor' and after a few weeks of perfunctory training I was let loose on the public with my false information and ignorance. At the time the chairman, Christopher Rodriguez, was playing fast and loose with the organisation as he turned it into a bank. He wanted to join the party in the city, and an expensive party it turned out to be, especially for the taxpayer who ended up with a thirty billion quid bill when the bank went bust.

But that's another story.

Fast forward to 2015 and the Michael Page employment agency rang saying they had a job for me. Not only was it a job, it was a job where I could use my knowledge of French, in fact I'd officially be called a linguist. Intrigued, I went to the their offices in central Leeds to find out more.

Leeds had changed a lot. I remembered it back in the eighties when it was full of rough pubs, grotty backstreets, and greasy spoon cafés. Now the city centre was firmly part of the neo-liberal brave new world. Urgent bearded young men strode purposefully checking their gadgets, mega coffee chains were everywhere, craft ale bars sold beer at five quid a pint. It was all an illusion, of course, because once you leave the sanitised city centre it doesn't take long to discover the crime, poverty and despair that blights so many of our major conurbations.

My interview was due to take place in one of the spanking new Wharefside developments overlooking the river Aire. In the 1920s riverside areas such as Hunslet were the cradle of the industrial revolution. Now the area has been christened 'Hunslet village' and had its eyes firmly planted on the proposed HS2 integrated station just over the water. Eight thousand more apartments are planned in this 'vibrant, mixed-use development' to quote the propaganda

5

puff piece from Leeds council. The industrial buildings that do remain now host high end restaurants and offices for the so called 'creative industries'.

And the offices of Michael Page.

Michael Page employment agency started in the mid seventies as a two man operation above a laundrette. It's now a global operation with over seven thousand employees. Michael himself has long retired to the golf courses of Portugal and Caribbean cruises but his name survives, emblazoned across every available orifice of the company. Inside the *Michael Page* office young, thin, and attractive Alice was friendliness personified as she left me in a room with a pile of forms which she asked me to fill in. As I sat there with my *Michael Page* pen, drinking coffee from my *Michael Page* mug, I couldn't help but think this was my first test. Maybe a bank of cameras were secretly analysing my body language the way they do in police interview rooms. Who knows? Why not? Anything, I felt, was possible in this airless, corporate, building.

After twenty minutes Alice bounced back into the room and spoke to me the way she probably speaks to her dad when explaining how to use a computer. Then she cut to the chase. The job, Alice said, was for a car breakdown company called *Green Flag* and we'd be helping English tourists who'd broken down in France. It would be on a six month contract, the pay £17,000 a year *pro rata*. I filled in the forms, told her I was interested, and forgot all about it. Then, about a week later, Alice rang and told me *Green Flag* had invited me to an interview.

Into the abyss

The *Green Flag* building straddled a major roundabout in the Leeds suburb of Pudsey next to a road sign announcing that Harrogate was eighteen and three quarter miles to the north. Very precise. Dawson's corner, as the area was known, was devoid of facilities except for an incongruous train station and bustling roundabout with a never ending supply of traffic. Sandy's sandwich bar opposite had an awkwardly placed metallic table with two matching chairs, not the most salubrious of places to leisurely sit with a sandwich and cup of tea. I peered inside. There was no sign of Sandy herself, just a hassled group of call centre workers with lanyards waiting impatiently for their fare to arrive. Amongst the items on offer was a *prawn marie rose salad.* Like Coronation chicken, it sounded like a throwback to the bad days of British Rail catering. I knew I was no longer in Bradford because a sausage 'barm cake' was also on offer, in other words a sausage sandwich but with an upwardly mobile Leeds twist.

The sandstone *Green Flag* building was part of a major complex of functional modernist workplaces with blacked out windows and a car park displaying an expensive array of cars. I looked long and hard at this daunting corporate edifice. Through the windows I could make out strip lights and see the occasional huddled figure working at a desk. I was early so I walked the full circumference of the complex to kill time. Next door was another call centre for a major bank, also constructed with corporate functionalism in mind. Outside people lanyard clad people trudged wearily to Sandy's sandwich shop for their break. A young Asian man paced the pavement as he spoke urgently to his girlfriend on his phone. A couple of disparate, overweight looking individuals tugged deeply on their cigarettes. When I peered into the complex itself I noticed a smoking area which looked like a bicycle shed spilt in two. Inside this rather forlorn looking construction people guiltily partook of their expensive and clearly frowned upon pleasure, outcasts and lepers confined to their dark green holding cage providing the minimum of comfort and shelter. Another red bricked edifice was slightly set back, again constructed in red sandstone, but with much more security.

It was guarded by a car bomb stopping barrier that popped up from the road and staff could only enter through an oppressive metal turnstile. A sign warned that tailgating was strictly forbidden.

In the middle distance I could see countryside, woods, fields and I suddenly had an urge to walk, to forget my appointment, to walk to the freedom beyond. But I needed the money so after taking a deep breath I went into reception and presented myself to the security guard behind a desk. Like Orpheus going into the underworld I'd crossed the threshold, crossed into the total control world of *Green Flag.*

Competences

After five minutes a Chinese looking woman with a broad Yorkshire accent appeared and led me into the beating heart of the building. Lines of people in headphones gabbled away in small telephonic booths. LED screens displayed meaningless numbers above. Whiteboards were arranged at the side of each cohort of workers containing names, numbers and word combinations that meant nothing to me. Nobody paid me any attention, so seemingly engrossed were they in their conversations. The room was festooned with *Green Flag* advertising slogans most noticeable of which was that of an actor in a petrol station looking for his girlfriend in the pouring rain. I recognised it from a recent *Green Flag* TV advertising campaign as well and the celebrated *Green Flag* dog also featured prominently. I noticed that the whiteboards at the end of each cohort contained the hastily written names of each worker and after each name was a comment of praise or shame. It truly was an alien world.

The Chinese/Yorkshire woman led me into a glass fronted room and began with an overview of what I'd been doing for the last year. I'd been living on my savings and writing a book. I told her, however, that I thought it was now time for me to 're-integrate' myself back into the working environment and improve my 'skill-set'. All bullshit of course. What I really needed was the money, but as an initial gambit it seemed to go down well. The interview then lasted for a gruelling two and a half hours, the main part focusing on so-called 'competences', hypothetical questions based on hypothetical situations to which you had to give hypothetical answers. They're an increasingly popular way of predicting a candidate's future performance, behavioural questions which ask you to describe a situation which demonstrates your abilities for the role you are being interviewed for.

'If a member of your team was struggling with their workload what would you do?' asked the woman reading from a pre-prepared sheet. What would I do? Maybe perk them up with a quick pep talk? Bollock them for letting the team down? I didn't know what the 'correct' answer was so I said something along the lines that I'd ask them if they were alright and make them a nice cup of tea. She furiously scribbled down my replies as I struggled to keep a straight face. 'Can you tell me about a time when you delivered excellent customer service?' How do you answer a question like that? 'I *always* deliver excellent customer service' I replied somewhat smugly, knowing it was complete nonsense. On and on these questions went until in the end I didn't care whether I'd got the job or not. I just wanted to get out of that oppressive building. Almost as an afterthought a Frenchwoman rang from another room to put my French to the test, she playing the role of a fusty garage owner in the Dordogne, me the role of call centre operative. Eventually after three hours, dazed, tired, and in desperate need of a pint, I handed back my visitors pass and staggered out of the sand red building.

A Green light

"If I was to tell you that _Green Flag_ would like you to work for them what would you say?"

It was Alice on the phone the following week. I was in the pub lamenting with my flatmate about the impossibility of getting a job with a corporate giant.

"Well, I'd say..."

Alice awaited my reply. I was like that guy on that old _del Monte_ advert as he decides whether a banana is of satisfying quality or not.

"...I'd say _yes!_"

"That's fantastic Michael" gushed Alice

"because _Green Flag_ really like you and they'd very much like you to join their team"

A wave of fear and euphoria swept through me. Somebody likes me? Why shouldn't I be flattered? Alice then made a quick mental calculation.

"If you wish to take the pension it works out at £15,720 pro rata. If you wish to opt out, however, it's £17,360. What would you like to do? Would you like to take the cash?"

She was sounding like Jim Bowen on Bullseye and I felt like a postman from Doncaster being given the opportunity to gamble my winnings away for the chance of a useless speedboat. In fact a number of thoughts swept through my mind regarding my lack of pension provision. At my age unless I win the lottery, rob a bank, or get left an eighteen bedroom mansion by a long forgotten great aunt they'll probably have to scrape me from the streets once I hit seventy.

"I'd like to take the cash!" I shouted out to Alice

"Great!" Alice shouted back.

"we'll send you the details online. Fantastic. Great news. *Well done*"

But accepting the job wasn't easy. In fact, it was tortuously difficult. An email arrived with a block of attachments and passwords, each password leading down a labyrinthine path that theoretically lead to an icon asking me whether I accepted the job or not. It felt like another test, inputting all these passwords containing letters, semi colons, hyphens, lower case dashes and incongruous numbers. My computer simply couldn't cope, I couldn't cope, so I put the whole thing off for a week, dreading the moment I'd have to re-open the emails and try again. Eventually I asked a younger, computer savvy friend, to help and after a complicated series of cut and pastes she discovered an icon that simply asked 'do you accept the job, yes or no?'. Why couldn't they have just rung me up and asked the same question? Anyway, I clicked yes and thought that was it. But it wasn't. Now I had to attach every certificate I'd ever possessed in my life onto a *JPEG* file, including three proofs of address, two proofs of identity and a number of other deeply irritating items which were difficult to find. It felt like I was doing all the work while *Green Flag* were simply sitting back and sending out lots of emails. I didn't have a scanner at home, I didn't have a printer either, so eventually I went to a printing shop, threw some money at the owner, and told him to make the problem go away. Thankfully he did and a few days later a simple email arrived telling me to report to the *Green Flag* training centre on Monday the 30th March at 9am. It was official. I was now a full time employee of *Green Flag*

Into the belly of the beast

At 8.52 on Monday the 30th March I presented myself at the *Green Flag* training centre, a bland, functional building opposite the main *Green Flag* headquarters. Internal doors could only be opened by the ubiquitous lanyards which were soon hanging around our necks and in the training room two banks of phones faced each other while at the front a well used whiteboard dominated. Outside in a stark recreation area a machine served free, sludge like, coffee. A second machine sold overpriced sugary drinks and unhealthy calorie filled snacks. We were an odd bunch that Monday morning in a suburb of Leeds. There was Monique, a French woman of a certain age who'd come to Yorkshire in the sixties to work in the wool trade. Despite the fact that Monique had lived in Yorkshire for over fifty years she still spoke English with the most outrageous of *'Allo.Allo'* accents, producing stifled giggles and ensuring heads turned every time she opened her mouth. There was Juan, a small, perpetually worried looking Spaniard who'd learned French working for *Medecin sans Frontiers* in Africa. There were a couple of African women, one an zealotical Christian with whom conversations could go dramatically wrong, the other a friendly lady with three

18

kids whose husband worked all hours God sent. There was an edgy, chain smoking, Parisian ex-chef called Paul who lived on a diet of Mars bars, hand rolled fags and crisps and there was also a cheeky young Mauritian girl with a coquettish smile. And then there was Claude, a big, black Congolese guy, the nightclubbing epitome of Mr Cool, who immediately sat close to my right, so that I could act as a human shield as he fiddled with his iphone.

A short, frumpy woman now entered the room.

"Hello everybody" said Judy.

"Glad to see everybody is *on time*"

Judy was flanked by an exhausted, mole-like man, who looked in desperate need of a good night's sleep.

"And this is Dennis" continued Judy

"he'll be training the linguists too"

Linguists.

19

I liked the title.

A French linguist.

It sounded sophisticated, high level, exotic, romantic. Yet any romantic notions about the job were soon dispelled when we turned on our screens and the training began.

But first it was time for a history lesson.

Green Flag, Judy told us, began in 1971 when a group of friends in a Bradford pub decided they could organise car rescue better than the AA. One of the friends owned a fish and chip shop and that's where the business began. Back then the AA and RAC were well established and offered assistance by the road but the *National Breakdown and Recovery Club* (as it was originally known) offered something different; a network of garages and mechanics that would recover and fix your car. When the service began, membership only covered breakdowns within a 50 mile radius of Bradford, and cost the equivalent of £1.50 a year. From such modest beginnings the company had grown into a car rescue behemoth, now even challenging the giants of the car rescue business themselves. *National Breakdown* became *Green Flag* in 1994 and, positively glowing with pride, Judy told us how 'we'd' sponsored the England football team in 1996 and the World Cup squad of 1998. She then cooed at the *Green Flag* dog before breathlessly telling us that the *Green Flag* HQ had been opened by Lady Diana Spencer herself in 1989. Why Lady Diana Spencer had been roped into opening such a bland, corporate edifice I'll never know. Judy said that *Green Flag* was one big, happy, family, a family she was proud to have been part of for the last 14 years. As Judy gushed away the mole-like Dennis perplexedly blinked, his heavily bagged eyes betraying decades of poor sleeping patterns, long shifts and mundane work. In a previous life, Dennis explained, he'd been a comprehensive school teacher, as his decibel ringing admonishments demonstrated. It didn't help that he was also deaf in one ear meaning he could bellow at the top of his voice safe in the knowledge that he was the only one in the room who couldn't hear the sound of his voice. Dennis explained that he normally worked nights but had been seconded in to help run the European training session. It was an offer, one felt, that he could not refuse. Then, after finishing her presentation, Judy told us to take five minute break and that the man in charge of that years linguists was on his way to give an introductory speech.

Enter Brian

Brian bounced into the room to a general series of hellos, a thick upper frame bulging incongruously out of his 57 year old body. Incredibly Brian had worked at *Green Flag* for over 35 years. An urgent, attack dog of a man, Brian started off by telling us that this years 'summer season' was 'his baby' and that he was determined nothing would go wrong.

Period.

The bulging frame underneath the unfashionable short sleeved shirt was evidence of extensive workouts in the gym, the lanyard around his neck merging into his body as if part of his anatomy. His thin moustache and steel rimmed glasses made him look like a part-time Nazi brown shirt. As we sat in cowed silence he laid down the law. Any lateness would be punished. If we *were* potentially going to be late we had to immediately ring him at which stage we were ordered to punch his mobile number into our phones.

Sickness was forbidden.

If you *were* ill, and Brian more or less implied he hadn't been ill for 35 years, you still had to come in anyway because there was 'always something we'll find you to do'. As Brian paced and lectured, Judy and Dennis looked on in stern faced silence. Any use of Hotmail or Facebook on the premises was strictly forbidden, along with our mobile phones, which we were now ordered to turn off and place into the nether regions of our bags. We were *Green Flag* people now and Brian was in charge, not just of our actions, *but of our very thoughts.* Finally his terrifying lecture finished at which stage he distributed sweets, wished us well, and went back to 'the other place' promising, *nay vowing,* to keep a very close eye on us indeed. It was now time to be introduced to the strange, lexical, world of *Green Flag.*

Losing the will to live

Booklets were distributed which explained the codes for different kinds of car breakdown scenarios. *COWS* (cut out won't start), *KLIC* (keys left in car), *KLIB* (keys left in boot), *NOFUEL* meaning the driver had run out of petrol, *MISFUEL* meaning they'd put the wrong kind of fuel in their tank. There were hundreds of these codes to learn and endless potential scenarios we might have to cope with. By the end of the first day's training session I was shattered.

The stifling conformity, the brain frazzling strip lights and strictly observed half hour lunch break meant that by nine in the evening I fell into a deep, strangely tormented, sleep.

As the first week progressed more passwords followed. Passwords to access European faxes, passwords to access our wage slips, passwords to open our dedicated internal complaints file. All the passwords ultimately gave access to the *Green Flag* internal computer system *POCWES*, or *Providing Our Customers With Excellent Service,* if we needed to remind ourselves of its name. *POCWES* was the great lumbering brain of *Green Flag,* the ever churning software of the entire organisation. But *POCWES* often crashed leaving us twiddling our thumbs while Dennis and Judy made a series of frantic phone calls to Brian. In the end I wrote all my passwords down on the inside of an exercise book, like ancient hieroglyphics, crossed out and corrected as each password became defunct only to be replaced by another. And this was only the domestic stuff we were learning. It was slowly broken to us that the European aspect of the job wouldn't kick off until late July, two and a half months away, so like so many other people in the country I was now officially working in a modern day call centre. In week two a second wave of linguists arrived meaning that there were now eighteen temporary French linguists at *Green Flag,* a subversive nucleus trained for elite activity on the main floor. But first it was time to party because we were now all invited to the annual *Green Flag* bash, our first chance to squeeze the flesh and impress.

A night at the ball

The bash was taking place at a nearby country house hotel. A smug and chubby boss acted as MC for the evening and awards were distributed for the most 'inspirational' team leader, 'step-up' team leader, and most 'improved' team leader. Dennis got a gong, as did Judy, as the top brass circulated benevolently around the room. The whole event took place with a studied, self conscious, air. Rictus grins prevailed. Nobody dare let their hair down, or, God forbid, make a fool of themselves. At the beginning of the evening Dennis sat at our table but was soon ordered, like a naughty schoolboy, to sit with the top bosses where they could keep a close eye on him. Not that any of this mattered to the linguists. We didn't know any of the movers and shakers, the faces to look out for, the faces to fear. We were only on a six month contract after which we'd all be getting the proverbial boot. *We assumed.* Intimations were already being bandied about that a few linguists from the previous years intake had been 'kept on'. The carrot was already being dangled.

A photographer then arrived and, like premiership players in front of an advertising backdrop, various teams were snapped with their respective supervisors. Prizes were held aloft, party poppers pulled and streamers launched, creating

27

an illusion of all-in-it-together egalitarianism in a distinctly unequal world. Eventually the second group of linguists hit the dance floor and as the evening wound down, so did the tension, until eventually the *Green Flag* control regime melted away. Yet, as 10.30 approached, people began to melt away too. Tomorrow was, after all, a working day.

When I got home I had to pinch myself wondering if the whole thing had happened. It had been an absurd, almost dystopian evening. If purgatory does exist it's probably like being trapped in a *Green Flag* corporate bash forever and eternity. But there was no time to think. It was already past midnight. In the morning I'd be back in the training centre for another gruelling day of *COWS*, *KLIB* and *POCWES*, another gruelling day of training documents, sludge like coffee and mind crushing tedium. But then we were invited to another corporate event, the *Green Flag* road show.

The rally

The road show was taking place in Pudsey civic centre
opposite the main building and we were all politely invited
to attend. At two o'clock groups of galley slaves drifted out
of the main building and assembled on the lawn flanked by
their team leaders. With time to kill I took a look inside the
civic centre. A noticeboard advertised Weight Watchers
meetings every Tuesday along with a 'toy and train' fare
and 'dancing for Parkinsons' classes. A plaque celebrated
the day the civic centre was opened on 12 April, 1972 by a
certain Alderman Oswald Lennon Walker, a rather lofty
sounding local figure. To the right of the plaque a door led
to the 'Owlcoates restaurant and bar'. To the left was the
main ballroom where the road show was to take place.

The top brass of *Green Flag* were in town, la *crème de la
crème*. It was a beautiful summer's day for the beautiful
people of *Green Flag*. Inside we were offered pre-rally

cups of tea, coffee, orange juice and - for some unknown reason - bags of monster munches. Then, at an unknown signal, all eighteen linguists were guided to the front row by Dennis, unwilling cheerleaders forced to fill the ranks. As we sat waiting for the show to begin I looked up at the stage. Inane, motivational, neo-liberal slogans were displayed on large placards. Centre stage was a huge, cardboard rocket divided into eight component parts, each part containing more inane statements such as 'growth' 'excellent customer service', 'task focused' and 'new direction'. Then, to the accompaniment of loud, booming, music the *Green Flag* top brass filed out onto the stage. As glitter cascaded from two strategically placed funnels Shaun Manning, *Green Flag's* head honcho, lead the way. Manning was the epitome of rockabilly corporate chic, with his fetching Elvis quiff and tie-less checked shirt. Apparently he'd worked his way to the top after starting on the phones, a remarkable achievement if true, and as he spoke I couldn't help but reflect on what a ruthless bastard he must be. In his jeans and tassled loafers he was hippy capitalism personified, exploitation with a smile, talking sweet matey slogans yet in reality just another footsie 500 boot boy wringing out every last penny from the assembled ranks. To his right stood a blonde woman with a rictus smile and heart of ice, to his left a spoilt looking chap with an overfed face who reminded me of that obnoxious, putty faced, judge on the *Dragon's Den*. At the far end two more *Green Flag* top brass were introduced, one a bald and sinister looking economist, the other a chubby, clubbable cockney who you could probably get pissed with at the local golf club.

But first it was the turn of an inspirational speaker who played a tape recording of an American call centre worker who'd 'gone the extra mile'. The tape, called the 'pizza test' featured a customer ringing a call centre and asking where they could get a good pizza. After telling the customer they were actually ringing a bank the call centre worker then 'goes the extra mile' by ordering the customer a pizza anyway, even asking what toppings he would like. It was utter bullshit of course yet when the recording ended the inspirational speaker said it was a perfect example of 'excellent customer service'. Eyes rolled in terrified silence but nobody dare demur. For two more mind numbing hours the show went on like this. More slogans, more charts, more glitter. There was even a silly quiz with worthless gifts at the end (the dreaded *Green Flag* pooch being one of the prizes), the event eventually culminating in a tub-thumping speech by Manning in which he pronounced, somewhat desperately, that car rescue was 'really exciting'. I didn't know whether to laugh or cry. As a final cascade of glitter spurted from more huge funnels the *Green Flag* top brass filed out to prolonged applause. All that was missing, I thought, was for the slogan riddled rocket to take off and land directly on the RAC headquarters. Car rescue gone nuclear, dirty corporate tricks being taken to their logical conclusion.

"How did you enjoy it?" asked Dennis as we all filed out

"It was...*interesting*" I replied somewhat diplomatically

Churning on

Call centres are a mixture of high stress, low wages, rigid management, and draining emotional labour. The most telling aspect of call centre work, however, is the pervasive electronic surveillance. Their expansion has been impressive. In the US alone there are now estimated to be 47,000 call centres employing 2.7 million workers or 'agents' as they like to call them. In Europe the figures are almost the same with 45,000 call centres and 2.1 million employees. Over the last two decades IT costs have dropped dramatically. As a result call centres have become the norm. Even in run down American cities disposable mobile phones are easily available and in most third world countries cyber cafés can be found. Call centres have become an important element in the so-called 'communicative capitalism'. But never forget. This new form of capitalism must cost capital as little as possible ensuring that the call centre worker is a unit out of which every piece of psychological and physical wattage must be extracted. Progressive thinkers have called them digital sweatshops, others have compared them to Roman slave galleons. They're not far wrong. It's because of these conditions that call centres have exceptionally high levels of staff turnover or 'churn' as it is known. According to one recent global study call centres tend to lose a fifth of their employees throughout the year, exceptionally high for any form of business. One reason for this churn is that people see such jobs as a launching pad for other forms of employment, using call centre work to gain references or experience in the workplace. But another important reason for this 'churn' is that despite the long series of tests

34

required to gain such jobs the quality of work on offer simply doesn't merit the effort put into finding it. After the rigorous tests, interminable interviews and amount of paperwork it's often a huge disappointment to find that you're no more than a glorified galley slave performing the most banal of tasks. Yet this 'churn' can also be seen in another light. It's not only a form of career choice, it's also a form of resistance in this world of total surveillance and micro managed tyranny. Call centre workers don't strike, they're not allowed to, they simply down tools and leave the job.

Listening in

We continued to work our way through every domestic car rescue scenario possible yet there was still no sign of European work. Some picked up the technical aspects of the job quickly but I was one of the slowest, struggling to learn each computer permutation. Juan, the worried looking

Spaniard, was the best. His youth and software knowledge made him sail through the multiple choice tests we had to sit. I failed twice, only passing on a re-sit, the implication being that failure meant we'd be out of a job. It all added to the sense of urgency, the atmosphere of tension, the gladiatorial jousting between those who passed and swaggered into the recreation room and those who failed and had to perform a walk of shame back to their computer to sit the test again. It was my first taste of call centre social engineering. I thought again about the question I'd been asked at that initial interview: 'If a member of your team was struggling to cope *what would you do?'*.

Eventually it was time to go over to the main building and listen into calls from the public. Dennis gave us a pep talk before leading us to the main floor where discombobulated conversations echoed from the myriad telephonic hubs. I looked again at the whiteboards showing lists of names and statistics, as if each worker was a floating share on the footsie, But still the statistics meant nothing to me. I couldn't work out if someone had a high number next to their name it was good or whether a low number meant they were heading for the sack. Supervisors circulated, fire fighting enquiries, seeming happy, *too happy,* with their *faux,* we're-all-in-it-together demonstrations of solidarity with the slaves on the phones. Eventually Dennis led me to the middle of the main floor where he introduced me to the man I'd be shadowing for the next few hours. Martin had worked at *Green Flag* for fourteen years and was a consummate professional. A real life audio terminator, he dealt with, and ended, calls with ruthless efficiency. Martin's voice had all the right bathetic inflections; a laugh when appropriate at a customer's weak joke, a pained sigh when the customer had been let down, a sternness when the customer needed to be moved on, a sympathetic ear when the customer needed to vent. Martin wasn't a human being he was a call centre humanoid, a Frankenstein's monster of empathy and hard ball, of disappointing and cheerful news, of supreme emotional control and deep seething anger.

If anybody was capable of going into Green Flag with an AK47 it would be Martin.

But for today Martin was fine, playing the dutiful game, helping me along, and ensuring next month's pay check would be pumped into his bank account on time. A coterie of similar looking men sat around Martin, hunched, blinking, gollum like figures with stunted, call centre frames, pallid complexions and fast food paunches. These were men who'd long given up hope of leaving this place, men who knew that so long as the mortgage was paid they could coast it to retirement in ten or fifteen years. That dream of retirement was their coping mechanism, and in-between calls they'd talk about holidays requested, shift patterns declined, and the previous nights football results. But it was also a dangerous game they were playing. They were only as good as their last call, only as fallible as their last loss of self control. One, hobbling, avuncular figure, nearly lost his rag while I was there before regaining control and passing his call onto Martin. It's stressful dealing with the public, stressful to be nice to people who are *not nice to you*. The academic Hochschild first posited the term 'emotional labour' to describe cabin crew in the early 1980s. Hochschild observed that it was not always easy to suppress your own emotional reactions in order to project a friendly and confident manner to other people. The 'emotional labour' aspect of call centre work is, along with the constant monitoring, one of the most demanding aspects of the job. The other problem is that because the work is carried out by telephone the call centre worker is denied the chance to pick up on any of the facial and physical clues that a face to face meeting entails.

Over the next week I shadowed a number of different people. One day I was paired with a fat girl who chomped,

39

slurped and crunched her way through calls from an array of drinks and snacks lined up on her desk. This girl sat in fatties corner, surrounded by other fat women, led by a terrifying dragon of a team leader who stomped and huffed her way around the floor. Some of these women were real heffalumps, their bodies malformed from years of sitting and chomping in the same position, with huge out of proportion arses, low hanging breasts and flying saucer sized hips. When these women got up and went for a toilet break I couldn't help but marvel at their sheer size and ugliness, at the way they'd surrendered to a life moulded into a chair, wired to a headphone. One day a cheer went round fatties corner when a large bag of buns appeared, the calorific contents snatched excitedly by a series of puffy hands as the calls rained in. Another time I shadowed a Hindu bloke who sat in the largely Muslim corner of the room, the only non-Muslim in this self consciously pious enclave. He was a helpful bloke who rode well the barbed comments of the excitable Muslim men and surprisingly foul mouthed and gobby young Muslim girls. Next I shadowed a permatanned stalwart called Tracey who sat in the divorcees corner. These middle aged women were the real workhorses of Green Flag, taking a phenomenal amount of calls whilst still managing to talk about male strippers, holidays in Tenerife and boyfriends who were good at doing the guttering. Call centre work is overwhelmingly female. Most estimates show that around seventy per cent of workers are women. Some academics have argued that management deliberately target women because of their 'feminine' qualities of empathy and abilities in customer interaction. After observing these ladies in action on the phones they might not be far wrong. These women were the objects of desire for the young, testosterone fuelled bucks who treat the work space like a strutting mobile gym, showing off their abs, flexing their necks and parading their arses. Vain, dismissive, self obsessed and narcissistic, these guys saw themselves as a cut above the rest, turning up to work with a half chomped apple, bottle of mineral water and bag of workout gear. One of them looked like a walking steroid finding any excuse to leave his booth, saunter down the aisle and twerk his repulsive, muscle bound arse. And finally there were the flotsam and jetsam of *Green Flag*, those who didn't fall into any particular category. These people 'hot seated' all the time, moving around the floor, not part of any clique. The flotsam and jetsam just wanted a quiet life, just wanted to take the calls and avoid Brian's attention. The flotsam and jetsam quietly counted down the minutes until

the end of their shift at which point they'd log off and dart quickly out of the building without looking back.

Le travail

It was finally time for the European training led by the linguistic department's pin-up boy, Stephan. Slim, grizzled, and fashionably tattooed, Stephan spoke French in machine gun fashion, his accent making him sound like something out of a 1970's Gallic gangster flic. Working alongside him was Agnes, a thin, stylish Parisian who by a strange quirk of fate had ended up working in a northern call centre. Agnes was a 'step-up' team leader and I recognised her from the corporate bash where she'd received a prize. She'd started on the phones too but had been determined to escape. Becoming a 'step-up' team leader was the easiest way to do it.

At our first meeting Agnes made it clear that the joshing and joking was over and the real work was about to begin. The pair of them then darted through the various European scenarios at break neck speed. Information on European service providers, the name and location of French *departments,* the rules and regulations regarding motorway breakdowns in France. We learnt about *Meon Valley* the hotel booking company *Green Flag* used in France,

43

something that sounded like a cross between a euthanasia clinic and an indoor adventure holiday. They told us about the so called 'private treaty' between the customer and the local garage, learning the statement we had to read out to the hapless driver which more or less said that if they got skanked by a French garage owner it was bugger all to do with *Green Flag*. We went through the spending limits if the customer got stuck for the night and we also learnt how to get confirmation from a garage that a breakdown was sudden and unforeseen. Of course there were yet more codes and passwords to learn; *ACCOM* indicating that overnight accommodation was required, *PREPAT* meaning the customer was returning home without their car, *REPO* if the car was going to be scrapped. If no code was available for the breakdown scenario for no apparent reason we simply input *CLIASON* so the whole thing could be sorted out later. Eventually, in my laminated Green Flag folder, I wrote down all the codes and passwords I now had to learn.

Employer number 0506840 (that was easy)

user name 676385 (ok)

password 84907j/m (right, getting tricky)

WFO password – Baudin 31 (WFO..already forgot what it was)

OBVR password Baudin 12 (right..forgot what that was too)

Lotus password – Lotus 1234 (straightforward numbers I suppose but what then hell was Lotus?)

POCWES station ID – 32445342 (the evil squid system)

Rescue ID – 6454524 (no idea)

CMS complaints – Baudin 29 (completely lost me by now)

Memorable name - Hetty

Favourite colour – Blue (?)

POCWES username – MO0506840

Password – freedom 4 (please no more)

Database - OLTP

Summer ID – OBVR

And there were more, many more. Numbers, hyphens, dots, dashes, dedicated files, new files, old files, European files, passwords for holidays, for payslips, for shift patterns, it really was more than my brain could absorb.

Before we knew it our European training was over. We'd had joy, we'd had fun, we'd had seasons in the sun. It was now time to 'go live' in the unforgiving panopticon of the main building

Now it was for real.

Going live

As the main floor babbled with activity we were led to a meeting room for a final pep talk. For some reason it was stressful, the thought of having a real life customer on the phone while their car was broken down. But roving supervisors would be available at the raise of a hand, Dennis explained, and there was 'no shame' in putting up your hand and asking for help. Inevitably poor Dennis had been roped into this role too. When the pep talk ended we collected our headphones and under the watchful eyes of the gollums, the fatties, the Muslim beardies and attractive divorcees, we filed slowly to our positions. We were not like the rest. We were the European season, the fancy French speakers, the unknown quantity, the necessary evil recruited every summer to help _Green Flag_ get through the holiday period. We looked, _and felt_, different as we filed across the main floor that morning flanked by grizzled pin-up boy Stephan. But Brian was now everywhere, his attack

47

dog poise honed to perfection. But then I realised Brian was being watched too.

By Jed.

Jed. The golden boy of *Green Flag*. Like Shaun Manning, he'd also started on the phones, but was now firmly ensconced in the cool, airy, calm of the third floor from where he directed operations and analysed results. We'd had an audience with Jed at the beginning of the contract where, in his air conditioned office, he deigned to give us thirty minutes of his advice. Tall, thin, blonde, *ice cool,* Jed sat in studied calm, fingers intertwined, as he explained how this year's 'European season' was going to be 'really exciting'. Brian sat in reverential silence throughout. Jed in his mid thirties, the stellar supernova, the erstwhile new romantic rock God, the cool capitalist who could have risen through the ranks of whichever company he chose to work for. There was ice in Jed's veins, he was the assassin. Now we were in the main building he became a lurking

presence, saying nothing, *observing everything,* standing

grim reaper like at the edge of the floor as he brandished

the scythe of early dismissal.

Especially for anybody who refused to 'adhere'.

Bringing into line

Loosely translated the German word *Gleichschaltung*

means 'bringing into line' or 'adherence'. It was the process

of Nazification during which the Nazi's established a

system of totalitarian control and co-ordination over all

aspects of society. Strangely enough *adherence* was the

word *Green Flag* also used to control their employees. The

word was writ large on the internal spying system which

logged every call, every break, and every toilet visit we

took. Our phones were not simply phones, they were

technological snitches from which there was no escape.

Through our phones *Green Flag* knew what we were doing

at every moment of the day, our behaviour logged on a series of flow charts constantly monitored by Jed upstairs in his swivel chair with purring white kitten.

Logging onto the phone required the inputting of two separate passwords after which we had access to a series of options explaining what we were doing at any particular time of the day. '*Aftercall*' was the most popular button to press. You could go on *Aftercall* as you were tying up loose ends after dealing with a case. If you didn't press *Aftercall* straight away another call would arrive hot on the heels of the last leaving you floundering through your screen. But if you went on *Aftercall* too long Brian would soon appear and questions would be asked. *Admin* was an all encompassing button covering a whole host of time-wasting opportunities, as was *System Down.* If you pressed *System Down* you could always claim that *POCWES* wasn't working, something that happened with infuriating regularity. There was the *Meeting* button which was self-

50

explanatory as was *Lunch* which was eagerly pressed as the clock struck one. But it was *Comfort Break* that irritated me the most, introducing as it did American lexical nonsense into our sacred and ancient language. And the perversion of the English language didn't stop there. When we wanted to book holidays all dates were presented in the inverted American fashion too. The 6th of April was 6/4 the twelfth of July 7/12 and so on (sorry buddy Osama Bin Laden attacked the twin towers on 11/9!) It was almost as if the whole wretched *POCWES* system had been block bought from that great God of ugly fat kid revenge, Bill Gates himself.

At first when we wanted to book a holiday we simply went to Brian, asked him for date, and he said yes or no. That was it. Civilised. Simple. Convenient. But once we'd gone 'over the road' Brian washed his hands of the whole process. We now had to request our holidays from an oleaginous, evil giant squid internal website with its inverted date changing trickery. As long, that is, your password didn't time out.

Because then you had to ring India.

Brian was still sat there, maybe four or five feet away, but if your password timed out (which was often) when you wanted to organise a day off work you'd be routed through to someone in Bangalore who didn't have a clue who you, or *Green Flag,* were. But this did have its benefits. While you were spending hours on the phone trying to get through to a perplexed Indian call centre worker you could put your phone on *System Down* thus leaving Jed helpless in his panoctic, Orwellian, lair.

And then there was that fucking dog.

'*Oh my*' was the catchword of the *Green Flag* dog in the television advertising campaign. Some of the women at *Green Flag* genuinely identified with it and inane female giggles would reverberate across the floor whenever someone said *'Oh, my'* in a silly voice. These women saw the *Green Flag* dog as an innocent, cuddly, Labrador rather than the sub conscious invading, self suggestive, money making, opinion forming trojan horse of capitalist doublethink it really was. Social media had its purposes for *Green Flag*, and the cuddly dog often appeared in it, but social media could also be - to quote one team leader - the devil.

Especially if you wanted to keep your job at Green Flag.

Upstairs, presumably somewhere near Jed, an entire team of people word searched the internet twenty four hours a day looking for any reference to *Green Flag*. They especially monitored Facebook and Twitter and we were expressly forbidden to mention *Green Flag* on any of our social media posts.

Forbidden.

Verboten .

Interdit!

Panic would sweep through the building when a disgruntled customer bad mouthed *Green Flag* in a Facebook mention or irascible tweet and the men in black would be quickly on the case. Bad tweets scared the shit out of *Green Flag* making them genuinely scared. News of a bad tweet would bring Jed down from his Orwellian lair to the far side of the room where he'd whisper something into Brian 's ear. Brian would then charge around the floor like an starved Alsation guarding a dodgy scrapyard. And there was another enemy at *Green Flag* along with Facebook and Twitter.

Paper.

Yes, paper. We are a paperless working environment they'd repeat robot fashion as if it was something to be proud of. Paper was *passé*, paper was *so* twentieth century, why everything was online from your payslips to your P45. Paper was something for *you* to print off at *your* time and expense. But I didn't buy it. Paper is good, in fact people wanted paper all the time. To make notes on, to write down registration numbers, to doodle, to daydream, to be a functioning, pen brandishing, human being. Paper thus slowly infiltrated its way back into the working space, reluctantly offered to the Luddites who still wanted to use it. But the paper was placed within sight of Brian 's desk so every time I took a few sheets from the pile Brian would look up, would note, would think....think *why is Michael using paper?* Perhaps I should have gone onto twitter to complain or, better still, onto Facebook and made a sarcastic comment about Jed. Perhaps I should have *written* a letter to top dog Manning himself and given him a piece of my mind. Instead, of course, I got back to work and did nothing. Paper or no paper, however, we were constantly being told to 'set the customers expectations'.

Whenever you went to Brian with a query the first thing he'd ask is whether we'd 'set the customers expectations'.

All around the floor galley slaves were constantly being told to 'set the customers expectations' If, however, every attempt to 'set the customers expectations' failed and the customer was still not happy it all got a little more scary. Because then we'd have to *escalate*.

Escalate! *Escalate!*

Like a manic darlek the word was used when all attempts to mollify had been rebuffed. There was even a section on the screen you could press saying *escalate* at which point Jed and his evil Jedis would come running pelle melle across the floor. They were terrified that an escalated case might go on social media and become real news. If the customer requested that a complaint be escalated the team leader or manager in question had to take 'ownership' of that complaint. There was no escape. That was when a team leader had to 'step-up' and prove to Jed why they'd been allowed to escape the phones. *Green Flag* were particularly worried that an escalated case might reach the desk of the dreaded Prudential Regulation Authority (PRA). An organisation that regulates and supervises banks, building societies, and major investment firms it was created in 2012 by the Financial Services Act. It was a response to the feral behaviour of the grasping bankers and city spivs who ruined so many millions of lives. The aim of the PRA was to protect consumers. It must be working because the thought of the PRA getting involved certainly concentrated the minds of the *Green Flag* top brass. In fact *Green Flag* took the awkward customer, the customer who would potentially *escalate* a situation, very seriously indeed. This was also due to the fact that when a complaint was logged and letter sent out, the customer was automatically given Financial Ombudsman referral rights. The problem with this for Green Flag was that if the awkward customer decided to take up those rights each referral case cost *Green Flag* £500 a time. So any complaint had

immediately to be referred to 'customer relations',
especially if it fell into any of the following categories.

Where a complaint is re-opened (customer still brooding)

Written complaints (anything on paper can be devastating)

Data protection Act breach (more potential fines on the
way)

Media threat (the ghost of the Daily Mail always hovered)

Complaints from politicians/MPs (potentially messy)

Any complaints on a case where the customer is deceased.

Worse still for Brian, Jed and all the other control freaks
upstairs was that a complaint might reach the gilded desk of
Shaun Manning himself. Now that really concentrated their
collective minds.

The panopticon

A number of years ago a couple of academics called *Fernie and Metcalf* conducted a study of call centre work. It's worth looking at what they concluded. They likened call centres to farmyards, drawing an analogy with 'battery hens' and describing them as offices where 'individuals sat in tiny pig-pens'. Harsh maybe but as time went on at Green Flag I began to observe the similarity. Fernie and Metcalf's main criticism, however, was aimed at the management techniques employed at call centres, techniques I became increasingly used to as the job went on.

Jeremy Bentham was an English philosopher and social theorist who in 1791 came up with the idea of the Panopticon, a building where there was nowhere to hide, you could be observed from every possible part of the construction. 'A new mode of obtaining power of mind over mind in a quantity hitherto without example' as Bentham so succinctly put it. A number of American prisons have been constructed with this idea in mind, Stateville in Illinois being one of the finest examples. Jezza, I'm sure, would have been proud to see his ideas achieved on such a huge scale with the modern day call centre.

"All that is needed, then, is to place a supervisor in a central tower and to shut up in each cell, a worker. They are like so many cages, so many small theatres, in which each actor is alone, perfectly individualised and constantly visible. Visibility is a trap. Each individual is securely confined to a cell from which he is seen from the front by a supervisor: but the side walls prevent him from coming into contact with his companions. He is seen but he does not see; he is the object of information, this invisibility is the guarantee of order, there are no disorders, no theft, no coalitions, none of these distractions that slow down the rate of work, make it less perfect. In call centres the agents are constantly visible and the supervisor's power is 'rendered perfect'" as one academic study argued.

Green Flag was indeed a panopticon where there was no escape from the management. Due to the advent of technology they can tape all calls and carefully monitor and ensure output. In the old typing pools and offices where workers sat in line performing tedious and repetitive jobs the supervisor could watch you from a seat at the front. But there were still opportunities to shirk, to doodle, to dream even if only in your own internal world. But not in the technologically advanced, panoptic world of the call centre. Computers which are ostensibly there to help the worker, also prove to be merciless monitoring tools which ensure that work rates are carried out to the maximum of what the worker is emotionally and physically capable of.

One big huddle

All aspects of our work rate would be brought up and discussed at a weekly meetings or, to use Green Flag's sick making vernacular, our weekly 'huddles'. And these 'huddles' never took place in a room, no, they took place in a 'hub'. Nobody had meetings at _Green Flag_ any more (like paper 'meetings' were _sooo_ twentieth century) they had 'huddles' in 'hubs', yet another verbal antagonism that had wended its weary way across the Atlantic.

"Guy's we're having a huddle" a near delirious Agnes would shout at which point we'd all file off to a room. But as far as I was concerned it was a meeting, an old fashioned, boring, yawn inducing, meeting, no matter how cuddly and right-on they tried to make it sound. It was another sick making example of cuddly Ben and Jerry style capitalism, along with bosses who skate around the Google 'campus' high fiving workers as they play ping pong.

Calling it a 'huddle' sanitised its meaning, brought romance to a soulless encounter, infantalised not only the language but the thought processes of everybody involved. More doublespeak, more cynical verbal manipulation. Needless to say the only subject up for discussion in these 'huddles' was how to make more money for *Green Flag* and the masters of the universe upstairs.

But woe-betide if you took the piss.

Once I sarcastically shouted 'guys we're having a *huddle* in a *hub*' at which point Brian gave me a blank, knowing, look, his glassy eyes looking deeply into mine. My card was being marked. Then I landed in potentially big trouble when I entered a harmless and jokey missive into the *POCWES* evil squid.

Big, down wid' the hood, Claude had a saying which he repeated at least twenty times a day. 'Life is not easy' Claude would say in the drawl of a fifteen year old youth who hung around too many American shopping malls. *Life is not easy.* It became a bit of a running joke between the lot of us, a coping mechanism, an in-joke, an expression of individuality under the noses of the supervisors. Then one day Brian called me over, sat me down and handed me a sheet of paper.

From: GFAgentSagnir@greenflag.com

Sent: 17 July 2015. 14.38

To: Customer Assistance Team Leaders

Subject: Advisor Feedback – Daily

Team Leader: Brian Stark

Incident number: 150897

More information:

While setting up a task, the advisor used inappropriate language and format. If the customer was to request all the information held about this incidence, this task can be seen as being unprofessional. English: "LIFE IS NOT EASY but please chase faxes regarding the customers breakdown in Limoges"

Sent from the Rescue Feedback Forms database.

I looked up from the sheet of paper. Brian gave me a silent, glassy eyed, stare. He said nothing, he didn't have to. I returned silently to my seat and went on *available*.

Brian the Darwinian

When the second group of linguists joined us a power shift occurred. Brian and Agnes now began to dangle overtime opportunities, all eagerly snatched by the young, Stakhanovisitic, elements both as a badge of honour and sign of devotion.

Stakhanov became a celebrity in Russia in 1935 during a campaign intended to increase worker productivity. A jack-hammer operator in a mine it was claimed he once mined over 200 tonnes of coal in a single shift and he was

65

awarded the Order of Lenin and Order of Red Banner for Labour. The legendary output of Stakhanov was used ruthlessly by Stalin as a way to shame workers into working even more. People genuinely bought into it, either through fear or through slavish devotion to the regime. Stakhanov even appeared on the cover of *Time* magazine, quite a coup for the Soviet propaganda machine at the time. The mythological output of Stakhanov and his towering example was a great way to sort out the wheat from the chaff, not only in the mines but in every other aspect during Stalin's dreaded five year plans. Like Josef Stalin, Brian was now in the process of sorting out the wheat from the chaff too, the goats from the sheep, the shirkers from the workers. Grouped together in the bottom corner of the main floor the linguists now became a kind of Darwinian experiment for Brian, our behaviour and performance monitored and watched in minute detail. Every job we did contained a time line and footprint (as the 'life is not easy' quip proved) ensuring that all mistakes could be ultimately traced back to the culprit. There was nowhere to hide at *Green Flag* and I was making mistakes. Not on the phone, but on the absurdly difficult series of screens we had to negotiate through. Not logging jobs correctly, setting dates for tasks that had already been done. Little mistakes in the scheme of things, but mistakes that were now picked up by the wild hounds in the linguistic team who were working every hour of overtime and were out to impress. Who knows, if you show willing they might even extend the contract at the end? That was becoming the great whispered question, the elephant in the room, the carrot Brian increasingly dangled as our fixed term contract approached its end. The wild hounds coveted that contract extension and were keen to keep on the right side of Brian. So when I made a mistake my name would be publicly called out by the young bucks. This wasn't just snitching, this was outright treachery. After just two months at *Green Flag* the

67

young bucks were behaving like major shareholders in the company rather than the overworked galley slaves with a limited shelf life they actually were. A little gang of workaholic young men now formed who'd mock and poke fun at me, shout out my name and laugh, something that didn't go unnoticed by the all seeing and all hearing Brian. Ironically the leader of this grovelling, cap doffing, arse licking gang, was Mr loverman himself Claude. Who'd have thought it? Big, black, cool, down with the hood, all night partying Claude. And not only was Claude managing to cast a critical eye over my workload he was even managing to shoot the breeze with the assassin himself, Jed. At the commencement of each shift the pair of them would now intertwine hands, twirl thumbs and cluck contentedly about their favourite steroid pumped, Ukrainian cage fighter. Who knows how far Claude might go? Who knows what Claude might say to Jed *about*

Brian? We were all in the big brother panopticon waiting to be voted out.

The romper room

After a month it was time for our individual assessments with Brian and Agnes which were to take place in one of the glass fronted rooms in full view of the work floor. From where we were sat we could observe the nodding heads, the studied inquisition, the examining of charts, the writing of notes. It made our collective imaginations run wild, each assessment culminating in Brian and Agnes performing a standing handshake after which the hapless galley slave had to perform a long walk back to their position. From the facial expression and gait of the person we tried to work out how the meeting had gone and whispered demands of 'how did it go?' and 'what did they say?' hissed through the air. Then it was my turn. The perp walk, the lonely procession to the glass fronted room oozing guilt and fear, all part of the plan, the plot, the theatrical, yet sinister, *IKEAesque* ergonomics of *Green Flag*. There was nowhere to hide at assessment time, no *Comfort Break* to press, no claim that the *System* had *Gone Down.* As I saw the outline of Brian and Agnes waiting for me through the glass partition a sense of fear and trepidation swept my way. Yet at first Brian was pleasantness personified, talking about the weather and asking me what my plans were for the weekend. As Agnes looked on, guarded and observant, Brian invited me to sit down.

He then gave me enough rope to hang myself.

'How' asked Brian inquisitively

'did I think I had performed in the last few months?'

Silence.

He tried again

'What' Brian continued, an air of studied curiosity on his face

'did I think my strengths and weaknesses were?'

The floor was mine.

The job, I said, had been 'interesting' especially with certain types of calls we received. What I really meant, of course, was that the job was repetitive, soul destroying and tediously boring. He knew that's what I meant, I knew that he knew that's what I meant. But never mind, the lying continued. I was, I said, 'relishing' the 'challenge' of working at *Green Flag* adding that I thought the job was 'improving my skillset'. So far so good. Brian liked that, I was singing from the *Green Flag* hymn sheet and as I spoke Agnes silently wrote down every word I said. (oddly enough *Green Flag* like old fashioned paper and pen when they're interrogating you!). But what were my weaknesses? I never really went into that, and deliberately so. Do turkeys vote for Christmas? I did blurt out something along the lines that I found it 'challenging' when *POCWES* went down, a remark that produced a quick, tormented, look between the pair of them. But other than that I kept my light firmly hidden under my bushel.

Then the interview took a more sinister turn.

'What' Brian now asked

'did I think of my fellow workers?'.

I was taken aback by his cheek, his noseyness, by his call to betray.

Brian's glassy eyes looked deeply into mine. Agnes's pen hung poised in the air. Outside rows of galley slaves peered curiously in.

'My fellow workers' I replied slowly, were 'OK'

But Brian wasn't happy with that. He wanted more, pulling me in closer, his cold and knowing eyes probing deeper

72

into my soul, eyes that had seen so many workers, so much human cargo, so much 'churn' through the years.

'But' Brian continued with a curious half shake of the head.

'are there any particular people who *stand out?*'.

Stand out?

I feigned misunderstanding and gave him a puzzled look.

"The linguists are..." I replied cautiously.

"...a very eclectic group. They *all* stand out at *Green Flag*".

Brian's thought processes came to a juddering halt. Agnes' red hot pen stalled in the air.

"A very eclectic group?" Brian slowly repeated the sentence to himself looking like he'd just swallowed a rare quails egg.

"Only you could have said that Michael...*only you*".

Then he let the dogs loose.

"On May the 21th you logged in 57 seconds late" said Agnes in a breathless Parisian accent. "On June 11th you were on *Admin* for three minutes thirty eight seconds. On June the 17th you took a *Comfort Break* of four minutes twelve seconds. Nine minutes later on the same day you took another *Comfort Break* of six minutes two seconds. On June 23rd you logged in one minute twelve seconds late, on June 27th you had another *Comfort Break* of five minutes thirty eight seconds. On average you have taken four minutes twenty eight seconds of *Comfort Breaks* a day"

The evidence stacked up against me was too great.

Agnes looked almost post coital after her breathlessly delivered accusations and I felt like handing her a cigarette. But there was now a long pause as Brian let me stew in my own shirking infamy.

"Could you tell me Michael." asked Brian with a puzzled and concerned look.

"do you think you might have some sort of *medical problem?*"

I looked at Brian .

I wanted to tell him to piss off.

I wanted to go upstairs and tell Jed to piss off too.

I wanted to unplug my phone and walk straight out of that building and into those hills.

Instead I said nothing.

"No, Brian" I replied

"not that I'm aware of"

"Good. Glad to hear that"

He was now standing, his hand outstretched.

"other than that everything's fine. Just take on board a few of the things we've said".

"What did they say" whispered the Mauritian girl as I made my way back to my seat.

"Oh, nothing" I replied

"they just said I was doing a good job"

Summer season kicks off

At long last we took our first European calls. And then a strange thing happened.

The phones stopped ringing.

It was like a truce, an armistice, as if shell fragments had been raining terrifyingly down only to be replaced by...silence. "You're in TX now' said Brian, meaning we had permission to go through the backlog of European jobs. It also meant we could go on *Admin* permanently. "Get cracking on those outstanding jobs before too many build up". We were now the officer class of *Green Flag,* drinking brandy in the mess while the grunts at the front went over the top.

But some of the European jobs were tortuously difficult to solve, cases stretching over weeks, even months, dealing with the slipstream of debris after a driving holiday through France had gone disastrously wrong. A lot of drivers didn't realise that rules on the French motorways are different from those in Britain. In France motorways are privately owned and the only people authorised to send assistance are the French police. Sending a *Green Flag* van to the rescue is not an option. Another aspect of driving often overlooked by the average English driver are the rules regarding tyres. In France all four tyres must be of the same brand, the same size, the same class of use and the same structure. Again this caused all kinds of problems when someone blew a tyre without a spare and had to wait for a replacement to be delivered from Paris, or even worse, from England.

Between May and the end of August France has a lot of long bank holiday weekends. Once two o'clock on the Friday of a bank holiday weekend comes French garage workers, taxi drivers, hire car specialists and everybody else necessary in getting you back on the road will have buggered off until Tuesday. Wild horses won't get them back to help you. 'But this is ridiculous' bellowed one man when I told him there were no hire cars, no garages and no taxis within an eighty mile radius for the next three days 'this wouldn't happen in Kent!' I had to break the news gently to him. 'but you're not in Kent sir, you're in France'. He sounded distinctly unconvinced after which he curled up into a ball, wept quietly and booked into a local *pension*. And wild horses won't get a French garage to open between 12 and 2. Without exception once the clock chimes twelve the whistling garage worker will take off his overalls, lock up the building and retire to a local restaurant with formica tables, jugs of local wine, and an appetising *plat de jour.* 'But this is outrageous, where are they all going?' shouted one driver at 11.58 just as he was on the cusp of getting his car fixed. 'Lunch, sir' I replied 'but they'll be back at two' . His reaction was predictable. 'but this wouldn't happen in Kent!'. Again, as on so many occasions, I had to remind the thrusting Anglo-Saxon male that Kent was not the centre of the universe and the world most certainly did not revolve around England. And, of course, nine times out of ten none of the garage workers spoke a word of English and none of the broken down drivers spoke a word of French. 'You can always get by with English, everybody speaks a bit' is often the riposte of a cocksure Englishman who's about to embark on a European adventure. This is the type of Englishman who has the impression that we still have an Empire on which the sun never sets. 'Everybody speaks English sir' I'd reply to this particular kind of customer 'apart from most of the people about twenty miles over the channel'.

One man claimed his car had been kidnapped by a French garage until he paid for the repairs. Another implied a three way conspiracy between the local *gendarmes,* hotels and garages leaving him trapped in a rural backwater for weeks. Vehicles with a low value often had to be scrapped to howls of impotent protest as it just wasn't worth bringing the vehicle back. At other times cars were held up for weeks as they waited for parts to arrive from England.

The grunts taking the domestic calls now cast covetous and sometimes furious glances our way as we sauntered up to Brian with our European based questions. On top of that we were speaking *French* a language Brian, Jed, and most of the other people on the floor couldn't understand. We were making hay while the sun shone, praying that the European based jobs didn't dry up. Yet by two in the afternoon they usually did. It was at this stage that Brian would re-appear and tell us we were "back in RX" meaning we had to re-join the ranks of galley slaves endlessly bombarded by domestic calls.

CUSTOMER:

Hello there, I've broken down, I'm not sure if -

GALLEY SLAVE:

Could I take your registration number please?

CUSTOMER:

I've got my policy number if that would help.

GALLEY SLAVE:

No, the registration number will do fine.

At this stage POCWES slowly grinds into action. Most of the time it will manage to find the customer but if it's a policy purchased through a bank you'll find nothing. But

lets assume their details have come up on the screen.

GALLEY SLAVE:

Could you confirm your name please?

CUSTOMER:

Peter Smith.

GALLEY SLAVE:

And could you confirm the make and model of your car?

CUSTOMER:

It's a blue Vauxhall Astra.

You move down the screen, click on an icon and pray that a

blue Vauxhall Astra in the name of Peter Smith comes up.

GALLEY SLAVE:

That's fine, Mr Smith, I've found your policy. So what's the

problem with your vehicle today?

CUSTOMER:

Well, I said to the wife this morning that we really needed some of those *Lidl* chutneys, so we got into the car and...

This part gets tricky. People often like to talk. What they have had for breakfast, how something like this has never happened before, how they were sure the car had a five year guaranty. But you have to control them, cut them short, because rambling customers are money down the drain for Green Flag. It's now that your people skills and cunning come in

CUSTOMER:

...*(three minutes later)*...and anyway as we drove into the car park...

GALLEY SLAVE: *(cutting him off)*

So your car won't start?

CUSTOMER:

Oh, er, no. It's completely dead.

GALLEY SLAVE:

It's not turning over?

CUSTOMER:

No, just dead. Nothing. As I was saying to the wife...

GALLEY SLAVE:

I'll just put you on hold a second, sorry about this.

Good tactic. Putting them on hold gave you a breathing space. It also meant you didn't have to listen to them whining on. But you couldn't put them on hold for too long. This might make the call stray too near the four minute fourteen second cut off time proscribed by the Green Flag boffins.

GALLEY SLAVE: *(taking customer back off hold)*

Sorry about that just a problem with our computer system.

POCWES was often used as a convenient whipping boy.

CUSTOMER:

I always having trouble with my computer at home you don't have to tell me.

GALLEY SLAVE:

Ha, ha, yes...they do make life complicated sometime.

(weak joke permitted)

Now could you tell me your exact location please?

It was now time to kill the call.

CUSTOMER:

Oh, er...well. Do you know that superstore?

GALLEY SLAVE:

Could you tell me which town you're in?

CUSTOMER:

Which town I'm in?

The four minute fourteen second limit is now looming. Jed is stirring upstairs. The meerkat like head of Brian is swivelling around.

GALLEY SLAVE:

Yes, which town you're in.

CUSTOMER:

Where I live you mean? Well I'm not there at the moment

GALLEY SLAVE:

Which town you are in at this exact moment. With your broken down car?

CUSTOMER:

Oh, with my car? Right now?

Yes, dumbkof

CUSTOMER:

Keighley.

GALLEY SLAVE:

And you said you were in the Lidl car park?

CUSTOMER:

Yes, that's right, because it's where my wife likes to go for

their chutney's and...

There's only one Lidl in Keighley. Time to kill the call

GALLEY SLAVE:

That's fine Mr Smith. Your policy includes a national

recovery which means that if we can't fix your car at the

roadside we will take you to a destination or garage of your

choice. We will endeavour to get to you within the hour.
Goodbye.

Hang up. Press Aftercall. Send task. Job done. Four minutes, three seconds. Thirteen seconds under. Brian and Jed are happy.

For now.

The Haven

But at least it was summer so in my precious one hour lunch break I'd go to a nearby meadow and lay in the sun. The sun's rays put the neurotic pressure cooker of *Green Flag* into perspective. From where I lay I could see the darkened windows of the building, the LED lights, the propaganda banner, the utter madness of moneymaking at full throttle. To stay in the building for the lunch break was sheer hell, the lighting, the stale air, the windows that wouldn't open, the *hubs*, the coffee machines, the TV propped high on a wall, the bean bag - yes a beanbag - used by hungover young men after a long night out. There was no joy, no laughter, no fun in that recreation room, just a constantly humming microwave, large TV, and the silent, mechanical, consumption of food. By now the Stakhavonites looked permanently exhausted. A few hundred quid a month extra in their pockets, yes, but they now possessed the tired, haunted look of the long term call centre worker. The Stakhavonites would stagger in for their breaks dazed from hours of telephonic conversation, numbed by the repetitiveness of the actions and requests, paranoid by the constant observation and criticisms. Yes, a few hundred pounds extra in their pay packets, but it was also twenty pieces of silver that ensured they'd become dependant on Brian's largess. They were now mere husks fully absorbed into the *gleichschaltung* of *Green Flag*. But sleeping in the sun was good. It rained only twice in all the lunchtimes I was there. God was giving me a break and lying in that meadow kept me sane. Once I pressed the

Lunch button on my phone I was free for that hour. Not even Brian, or Jed, could stop me from enjoying the sun.

The dull ache

By now, however, my arm was permanently aching. In fact my whole left side was, pins and needles in my elbow which spread up to my shoulder. At first I thought I might be having a stroke. What a way to go, I thought, collapsing at *Green Flag* under the pitiless gaze of Brian and Jed. But then I realised it was my posture that was causing it, the way I sat, the constant use of the mouse, *the whole bloody thing.*

After only three months working in a call centre I was getting RSI. RSI or *repetitive strain injury*, effects limbs and soft tissues of the hands, arms, shoulders and neck, a kind of inflammation of the sheath that surrounds a tendon. The best way to combat it is by adapting the correct posture and taking regular breaks, not easy to do when you're glued to a phone under constant surveillance. I'd met two people in my life who'd contracted *Repetitive Strain Injury.* One was a woman in her thirties who'd worked in an office all her life. They'd done tests, taken X-rays, performed MRI scans but there was nothing the doctors could do.

Nothing.

Incurable.

Then I met another bloke who suffered from it. Middle aged, worked all his life in an office too, rooted to a computer and a desk. Everything was going fine for him until one day he realised he had a pain in his arm, a niggling pain, a niggling pain that in the end never went away. Like the woman, he went to the doctor who told him the same story.

There was nothing they could do

And now it was happening to me.

But how did Martin the call terminator survive? He'd worked there fifteen years. How did the crunchie chomping heffalumps, the divorcees, the flotsam and jetsam, the people who'd been there six, seven, *ten* years. Why didn't they have RSI, the yuppie flu of the arm? I imagined the scoffing laughter of the builder, the fisherman, the fire fighter, the roofer, the men with real jobs. But they could scoff all they liked.

I was working in a call centre and my arm bloody hurt.

Yet still the Stakhavonites were on my back, those useful idiots, that unholy alliance of stupid young men mocking my work rate and criticizing my mistakes. Eventually I grasped the nettle and spoke to a couple of them individually. Of course they denied it, especially big Claude, who denied it loudly, *too loudly*, ensuring Brian's neck again jolted and swivelled above his desk. But I'd made my point, insisting that any future criticisms be sent as an internal email. Better still that they be made face to face out of earshot of Brian. Then I thought again of the searching question Brian had asked at the end of my first assessment.

'What do you think of your co-workers?' Brian had asked 'do any of them *stand out?'*

What, I thought, had Claude said about me?

The evil squid

It started with bad dreams. An inability to switch off. The longer the job went on the harder it was to simply switch off. Case files, unfinished jobs, criticisms followed me well into the night. But it was the dreams that started to get to me.

Dreams about Brian

In one I was writing on a notepad which Brian snatched away before looking sceptically through the contents. In another I had a pile of unfinished jobs and Brian angrily came my way with his nasty moustache, pitiless eyes and unnaturally large frame. I woke up with a jolt. When you start having bad dreams about your job, any job, it's time to get out. And I was no longer myself. As every day passed I was becoming more like *them,* talking in the royal 'we' about *Green Flag,* gradually possessing the same hunted look as all the rest. And then I realised. I was slowly beginning to 'adhere'. My mother noticed it, then close friends. The fact is I was stressed. I never had downtime any more, never had time to unwind. The conveyor belt of shifts, casework, calls, criticism, of lacerating self examination was now taking its toll. But most of all I had the sensation that I was being *watched*. All the time at *Green Flag* you knew you were being watched.

After four and half months I wanted out.

The great escape

I'd been saving my holidays with the intention of holding

out until the end of September when the contract finished.

The plan was to finish half way through September, take

my two accumulated weeks, and not come back. It was now

mid August. If I could just get through a few more weeks

I'd have virtually finished the job. But September now

looked a long way away. I'd forgotten what it was like to

clock watch in a job. I'd done it in the past, temping in

offices, sitting through tedious presentations, working in

classrooms, standing in car parks dressed in a fluorescent

jacket. But I was now clock watching at _Green Flag_ like in

no job I'd done before, counting every single minute until

the start of each break, until the end of each shift, until that

high pitched noise the phone emitted when you _Logged Off_

for the day. To add to all this another 'assessment' with

Brian and Agnes now loomed. What would they say?

Would they keep us on?

That was the big unanswered question, particularly amongst the Stakhavonites. By now they were used to the £1,232 pumped into their bank accounts on the 18th of every month. Add to that the extra two hundred quid from the overtime and they were now salary addicts, casting desperate glances at the dark uplands of October when the job, and the cash injection, would finish. Brian knew the Stakhavonites wanted to stay, that they'd taken on more financial commitments as the job progressed, that they now 'needed' that monthly wage. That was his power over them. I, however, wanted to go.

Then one Sunday I cracked.

It started when a customer rang saying he needed assistance. As usual I couldn't find his policy due to a problem with *POCWES* so I waved him through, sent assistance and forgot all about it. Two hours later, however, a woman rang on the internal phone, a bitch, a nasty piece of work, a humourless woman with frumpy clothes, bad hair, sexless marriage and a mission to make everybody else's life miserable.

"Can I speak to Michael?" said the bitch curtly.

A knot formed in my stomach. It was like being back at school.

"Yes, that's me"

'This is Dawn upstairs. Do you remember a Mr Parry in Halesowen?'

Dawn. Nasty, colourless, Dawn.

"You gave him service but his policy has clearly lapsed. Why did you do that?"

Why did I do that? Why do people do lot's of things Dawn? Why did Lady Diana Spencer get in the car when she could have stayed at the Ritz for the night? Why did a second shot come from the grassy knoll? Why did George W.

Bush ship his Saudi mates out as the twin towers collapsed?

Questions, questions, Dawn, questions.

"Did I?" I replied buying time

"give me his registration number and I'll look the case up"

I put the witch on hold.

But as I searched for Mr Parry's policy another woman from a different part of the building rang on the internal phone too. She worked for TST, the *Gestapo* of *Green Flag*, a secret, unseen, unit that monitored everything.

"Do you realise you've been on *Aftercall* for four minutes. *It's too long"* said the shrill voice of Debbie from TST.

'That's because I'm talking to Dawn upstairs"

"Four minutes is too long, go back on *Available*"

By now pop up emails were frantically raining in from Dawn asking why I'd kept her on *Hold* for so long

"Are you telling me to deal with Dawn later?"

"I'm saying that four minutes on *Hold* is too long"

Bitch number two hung up. I went back to bitch number one.

"I've been informed by Debbie in TST that I can no longer deal with your case" I said coldly "we have a huge volume of calls at the moment. If you want to speak to me about Mr Parry's policy send an internal email and we'll speak at an appropriate time".

I cut her off and went on *Comfort Break*. There was no way I was going to last until the end of September. In fact I decided to leave the next day.

The home run

The following morning Brian caught my eye as I sat at my desk.

"I was wondering" we said simultaneously

"could I have a *word?*"

The synchronization of our words and thoughts was uncanny. He handed me an envelope.

Dear Michael,

I write to inform you that you are required to attend a meeting to discuss the pending expiry of your fixed term contract on August 19th at 10.00 pm in meeting room 1.

The meeting will be attended by myself and Agnes Foucault.

During the meeting I will be discussing with you your (performance/attendance/conduct) during your employment. You should note the outcome of this meeting may result in the termination of your fixed term contract with us.

During the meeting you will be provided with the opportunity to discuss and respond to the points that have been raised. You have the right to be represented at this meeting either by a union representative or by a work college. Please refer to the disciplinary policy for

information on representative attendance. Please contact

me by Tuesday 18 August to confirm that you will be able

to attend on the date and time stated.

Your Sincerely

Brian Stark

"Could we have that meeting. *now?* " I asked.

Brian's meercat like head twisted my way. His glassy eyes looked searchingly into mine.

"Yes Michael, I think we can arrange that"

All the linguists looked on as I walked with Brian to the glass fronted interview room. Within two minutes of entering Brian cut to the chase.

"If I was to say to you that we would *not* be renewing your contract how would you feel?" asked Brian .

There was a pause.

"If I was to say to you that I'd like to leave tomorrow what would *you say*?" I replied.

Again, the synchronisation of our thought processes was almost eerie. I'd checked my bank balance. My £1,232 had arrived.

"I don't see a problem with that Michael" said Brian.

'I'll just have to confirm it with upstairs"

Upstairs meant Jed.

Brian left the room to make the call. On Brian 's desk I noticed my file laid out with a flowchart showing my *Comfort Breaks*, my lateness, *my Idle Time.* It was a file now destined for the bin.

'That's fine" said Brian returning breezily into the room. He looked as relieved as I did. We knew my working there any longer was a waste of time. We also knew that we didn't want to argue with each other. In no time at all we'd smoothed over the logistics of my departure and were

shaking hands.

'The thing is" I said to Brian as I went finally to the door.

Brian 's glassy eyes again looked deeply into mine

"the thing about this job is that from day one the end of our

contract has hung over us like a sword of Damocles'.

Brian thoughtfully stroked his chin,

"A sword of Damocles...." he slowly repeated aloud

"Only you could have said that Michael....*only you'*

My four and half months at *Green Flag* were over.

Printed in Poland
by Amazon Fulfillment
Poland Sp. z o.o., Wrocław